STEPHANIE STRANGE

Doing Our Damndest

more bullshit from Stephanie Strange

Copyright © 2023 by Stephanie Strange

All rights reserved. No part of this publication may be reproduced, stored or transmitted in any form or by any means, electronic, mechanical, photocopying, recording, scanning, or otherwise without written permission from the publisher. It is illegal to copy this book, post it to a website, or distribute it by any other means without permission.

First edition

This book was professionally typeset on Reedsy. Find out more at reedsy.com

Contents

Every Beginning is An End	1
Imaginary Fiends	3
Call to Order	6
Persephone's Song	8
Blame it on my ADD	10
Stars	18
Cartography School	19
My Car	20
Tomato Porn	24
Shush, A Gift	26
Upside Down and In the Dark	27
A Dirty Dozen Plus One	29
Leftovers	31
She Caught a Draft	32
A Jesus Guy	34
Pink Blankets and Black Aprons	37
Thing is	39
Hanger	41
Another Broken Mirror	42
Mouth Breather	45
Julio and the Ants	47
The Ice Queen	49
you paid for it	53
Story Witch	55

The Bunker	57
Splits and Splones	59
Nor Nary	60
Something in Common	62
Hard Boiled Afternoon	64
Pavlov's Bitches	68
Broken Edges	70
Even Then	72
A True Agnostic	74
Entertaining Thoughts	77
Things That Happen	82
A Flight	83
It Ain't Easy Being Prey	85
Sushi For Your Thought?	86
Red	88
Demetria's Sweaters	90
Losers	93
Cakes for the Lady	95
Cowboy Stuff	96
Rogue Agent	98
UV Gone Mad	100
32 Seconds with Jack	103
One Time Only	105
I, Eye	106
Falling Fruit Season	108
A Special SOB	110
The State of the Garden	111
Deviled Eggs	113
Reddy to Go	115
How Are You?	117
The suspiciously familiar song of the Marsh Wren	119

Another Poem About My Hair Leave Me Alone And I'll Stop...	121
Our Damndest	123
It's a Stranger World	124

Every Beginning is An End

This morning I woke up and decided I would write another book. Rather, that I would gather as many of my short memoirs and half poems as I could find, and fling them out into the universe, as far away from me as possible.

It's me.

I'm sitting in my nest with years and years of eggs that I've laid but never nurtured; brittle little corpses that I never pushed out for fear that they would splatter all over the ground. (Is anyone ever ready to be a mother?) So now it's just me and you and this army of fragile bones and hefty ghosts and a nest that chafes in all the wrong places.

It's awkward.

What follows is a collection of memoirs, poems, and rants from a child that never really grew up and all of the callousy moldy garish spiteful sad sweet scared rainbow layers that stand between us.

I'd like to dedicate this book to my Great Aunt Gracie, who I'm told was a real bitch.

She was also my first friend.

Imaginary Fiends

The market is not a person.

It can bear so much more than a person, because it's not real.

The market is my imaginary childhood friend, my deceased Great Aunt Gracie, who I never met.

She was a verbally abusive alcoholic who lived a hard life and walked into a fireplace one day. She lived a handful of years afterwards, her body covered in burns, her temperament understandably more vitriolic in her remaining years.

She yelled and abused and was invited over to dinner time and again because she was family, because she was troubled, because she had nobody else. She hurt the people who supported her. She called late at night to fling her poison onto persons softer and less scarred than herself.

I heard the stories, the worst parts no doubt left out for little pitchers, but when it came time for me to bring an imaginary friend into this world, for some reason I chose Gracie.

She wore a pink nightgown with white frill at the sleeves. She scowled and limped and was covered in red-black streaks from the fire, her face a mask of horror, with bits of shiny white bone peeking through. I made a bed for her on the floor out of blankets every night and she wasn't kind or unkind to me. She was just there, muttering under her breath and accepting what I gave her, an untrusting animal incapable of regret or reflection.

One day I heard my parents talking emotionally about taking me to therapy. They were upset about me and my elderly, burn-covered, invisible, once-living friend, so far outside of their realm of experience. I always worried about them, my parents, and did my best to keep them from worrying.

So I made a difficult decision and said goodbye to Gracie, my morbid companion, telling her that I wouldn't forget her. Still, sometimes I left bread and peas for her on my plate, giving her a little nod when nobody was looking. A secret smile. Something just between us. She mashed the peas into the bread and made it into a sad face sandwich which she devoured, making horrible and funny faces. Nobody but me knew what a clown she could be.

She disappeared around middle school, though sometimes I still see a pink flurry of movement out of the corner of my eye, but I no longer see the face burned to a horror movie crisp except in my memory. Sometimes I feel my anger crackling like the heat from a fire and I wonder if I understand her particular brand of poison; if maybe she wasn't the unlikeliest of companions after all.

All that is to say, the market is not a person, and can bear so much more than a person, because it's not real.

And I think you should just trust me on this one.

Call to Order

Every week I call the meeting to order.

The table is different every time and so is the room.

I wait patiently for them to show up.

The funhouse mirror reflections. The warped ones.

We find each other in the waiting room and I struggle to remove my blindfold.

Sometimes they show me things but mostly they don't because they love me so much.

Mostly it's crowded and sometimes it's sparse.

Sometimes we're in the red house but mostly they leave me to wait outside, where my sister and I try to understand each other under the chlorinated pool water.

No, I don't understand what you said. Let's try again.

CALL TO ORDER

And this was how we entertained ourselves.

There I am in the garden, naming stray cats, naming caterpillars.

The things I kept in order of appearance:

1: This understanding about names and their importance.

2: My blindfold.

We can't always get what we want. But if we walk into enough walls, sometimes we get what we need.

Persephone's Song

It had to happen eventually
    and what a long dark corridor it's been.

And how she waited all that time, coronation whites stained pomegranate red by the time she took the throne, the only thing she ever did slow. The only work she ever did show.

Would you call her a glutton that she ravished the seeds? Each pop pop pop satisfying the sigil holders at long last (talk about your insatiable appetites).

In the name of the Mother, the Daughter, and the Holy Witch. Amen.

We lift our veils and drape them across your marble statues with their cleft chins, 'this is for your own good' she whispers with her eyes as she ba badump bumps away, so you never even notice the slithering and the swishing and the grinding, a wonder when you dull the senses what jumps out at you. Nobody has hands like mother.

Shshsh, it's okay.

We know you're scared. Though you have not the words nor the capacity to say it.

You'll grow used to it.

You've no choice, for this will be a long swing of the pendulum. Easier on those who haven't been leaning on locked knee.

From the steeples they weep, knowing God prefers caves to pointed heights of hubris. They're confidential like that.

And our rose by every other name?

She's practically giving away blood like every day is Black Friday.

What a deal!

No takesies backsies darling.

It was writ in the stones and sealed by the stars.

Count yourself lucky that she's not so petty as you. And when you find yourself, safely in the fold, do remember to mind your manners.

Pleases and Thank you's can be worn long after Labor Day.

Everything fancy. Everything free.

Blame it on my ADD

This year for Christmas my mom got me a gift certificate for a facial.

Every year I tell her not to get me anything and every year she tells me not to be silly.

So we settled on a Groupon facial that wouldn't have her spending too much of her hard earned Uber money.

When I arrived at the appointment, I changed into a white drape and positioned myself on the table with a bolster under my knees. The esthetician put a bright white light on my face and started examining my skin and pulling out bottles. While she was massaging nice-smelling goops into my skin she asked me "When did you start to notice these broken capillaries on your left cheek?"

This was a typical facial. She would continuously ask me about my "problem areas" and then try to upsell me on a miracle cream or two that would make me beautiful by the time we were finished.

I told her that I hadn't paid it much attention. She persisted and asked me twice more, "Do you know WHEN this little area started to show signs of aging?"

I finally told her that I had noticed my general skin issues about four years ago, when I quit drinking.

That seemed to be enough to get her to stop asking stupid questions.

It was true though. When I quit drinking I felt like my face and body were falling apart. I was stressed out all the time and I suddenly noticed that I was looking older. I saw blotchy skin and noticed sun spots for the first time. I came to the conclusion that somehow alcohol had been the glue that was holding me together, and now that I was sober I was falling apart. In time I would realize that I just never looked too closely at my face in the fifteen years I had dedicated myself to drinking and tending to my opioid habit.

Sobriety brought about a painful new awareness in a lot of ways that felt crippling. The confidence I thought had been gifted to me by the Gods was eroding as new realizations about myself and the way I had been spending my time flooded and tiptoed in in wicked turns. From facing the realities of sexual promiscuity and being an asshole to people who tried to help me, to the scope of how poorly I had treated my physical body, I felt like a worthless sack of shit for a good long while.

These dark mental meanderings were coupled with wonderful new realizations that I didn't have to be like that anymore, and that I was extremely lucky considering the choices I had made. As I was facing my past, I was looking towards my future, and the whole thing was a real clusterfuck.

With my painful new awareness I learned, through trial and error, that this path was mine to walk alone. Nobody was equipped, able, or willing to walk this path with me. I mean…a therapist would have been good, but I didn't know that I was at the beginning of a long journey that would take me to some places where I would eventually need a hand or two. And I was broke, with shit insurance, scared and hopeful.

I tried to talk through this poison that was constantly working its way to the surface, but for *some* reason it made people uncomfortable when I started talking my way through the thorny difference between being a drunkly promiscuous young woman and being raped.

So when this esthetician asked me WHEN I started noticing my broken capillaries it seemed best to tell her that I started noticing them four years ago, when I quit drinking. It was easier than reporting from the front lines of my mental onslaught,

As soft music piped into the room I started thinking about all of the falls I had taken over the years. They were grouped in my memory in large vague pods, and occasionally one would break free. When I sobered up I hadn't expected memories to break free a full four years after quitting pills and drinking. I figured that the first year would be hard and then things would level out.

Which is hilarious.

As she picked up my hand and started massaging it I was suddenly engulfed in a memory.

Beaverton, OR. 2000-something. (I have no idea when, my timeline is all screwed up).

I lived in an apartment near the max (Portland's public transport). I had moved in with some friends from college after I dropped out. They had graduated but I couldn't keep up with classes due to my One-Day-Awake-Two-Day-Asleep schedule.

I had intended to find a job but never followed through. I managed to scrape together money every month by borrowing from my parents and selling some of my pills to friends. The friends who I had moved in with had moved out. I didn't know why and I didn't ask. I was living there alone but this was back when rent for a one bedroom apartment was in the $800 range. I swung it by the seat of my pants.

I spent my long days taking pills, drinking alcohol, watching television, eating, and sleeping off the alcohol and pills. I measured these days in what shows were on television, before streaming. Charmed started around 11AM, which was a good a reason as any to wake up. Then I had to power through two episodes of something inferior, maybe Law and Order, then two more episodes of Charmed followed by whatever movie was on. My whole day was mapped out this way.

Then the cable broke.

Where I couldn't manage to get dressed most days, I was able to immediately call the cable company and have someone sent out that afternoon, which left me with several hours to kill.

So I went out for a drink. Drinking in public was a real event at this point in my life. I put on clothes and left my filthy apartment with cat litter piled high against the wall and dirty dishes stored in the oven, and went to the bar around the corner. The day melted by as I sat there bullshitting with other drunks until I finally asked someone what time it was and realized I needed to be home NOW if I was gonna catch the cable guy.

I started for home, running and walking in spurts, desperate to get there in time so I wouldn't have to kill another day left alone with myself.

On the sidewalk there was a scooter lying on its side, with kids playing close by, screaming and laughing in their own joyful world. Without much thought I righted the scooter and hopped on it and started flying for home. And boy was I flying. I felt tingles through my body as the greyhounds I had been drinking and the pills combined to give me a euphoric feeling that bloomed somewhere between my chest and my stomach.

I could have actually been flying. I was a bird, soaring through the air. Perfectly free.

Until I hit a crack in the sidewalk. Then I was Really flying. In this new/old memory that was worming its way out as I was receiving a tender hand massage, I flew a whole city block before I landed square on the left side of my face and slid another few feet on the side of my face with signs of aging.

Luckily, I was as doped up as it's possible to be, so I felt no pain. Just dismay as I stood up with blood on my hands and clothes and continued running home, leaving the scooter in my wake.

My priorities were still intact. Get to the cable guy, then tend to the face. When I got there he was just pulling up and asked me worriedly if I was okay. I told him I was fine and laughed about my little spill as blood dripped onto the carpet and I wiped my hands on my jeans pretending that would fix me up. His worry silently shifted from me to his own well being as he took me in.

I excused myself while he worked on the cable to wash my face. From my eyebrow to my mouth there was plenty of blood and I was starting to swell up. The bulk of the cuts were just below my eye and on my upper left cheek. I checked my teeth, no chips. There was dirt from the sidewalk all jammed into the scrapes, so I did the only reasonable thing: I splashed some cold water on my face, gingerly dabbed it dry with a dirty towel, and popped two more methadone. I had reached my 6 pill/4 drink max already…anything past that and there was a chance I'd be sleeping and vomiting for the next three days, but this here was a special occasion. I felt excited that I had a legitimate reason to go past my self-imposed limits.

When I left the bathroom the cable guy was standing by the open doorway eager to be gone. He told me it was all fixed and I thanked him.

Blissfully alone again, I changed into pajamas and sat down in front of the television. This was where I wanted to be. Despite my heavily medicated state, I could feel my face throbbing under the fuzz. I didn't much care.

Gentle flute music came back into my awareness. As this stranger with the smelly goop creams moved to my feet for a foot massage, a few hot tears escaped from the corner of my eye, blending in with the gooey stuff on my face. I didn't even know why I was crying. I'd had many memories surface since I quit drinking, more so in recent years, some of them more painful than a stupid fall.

By the time she moved back to my face there was no trace of my few wayward teardrops. She finished up the facial, told me to put potatoes and yogurt on my face, said it was nice to meet me and didn't try to sell my any expensive creams. Which was kind of disappointing because I wanted something miraculous to slather on the left side of my face.

Later I would frame the story differently, telling my partner about the hilarious time that I stole a kid's scooter and scraped my face along the sidewalk when I was a fall down drunk, which is why the left side of my face was dying faster than the rest of me. We would laugh about it, because there's nothing else to do and also it's horribly funny in its way.

These moments take me away, when I'm suddenly drowning in a sea of wonder and regret.

Who was I?

Who am I?

Why did I waste so much of this short life?

If someone handed me pills would I become that person again? What is really different about me then and me now? There is barely anybody left in my life these days who knew who I was then…it could have been a bad dream but for these busted capillaries that the esthetician won't shut up about.

Throughout my week I get distracted in my conversations with people. I zone out for long stretches and joke that I have ADD. But the whole truth of it is I'm just somewhere else.

Mentally filing away new/old memories and trying not to react to them; grilling myself with the wrong questions that can't be answered and are not helpful to ask.

If this is what it's like in my head, how many other people are walking around with these worried hamsters spinning in their wheels, getting distracted and joking it off, wading neck deep through their own grey matter, more alone than we ever acknowledge?

But I like writing about this stuff. It gets the poison out quicker. It lets me laugh. It helps me get to the moral: Don't buy facials off Groupon.

Just kidding.

I don't know what the moral is.

Stars

Maybe we are like stars
    Moving away from each other
    At a pace that makes the glaciers melt with jealousy.
    All we'll have is the neighbor's porch light
    Further and farther away
    And that might be enough
    For a long time
      even though time gets shorter the longer you sit in it.

And I might seem a monkey on your back
    a fly in your ointment
    a metaphor in your mixed drink,
    But you'll miss me when I'm gone.
    and I'll miss you too.
    And that's what I meant when I said "I love you".

Cartography School

I went to cartography school and was told "This is how you make a map".

This one is all buggered up and it's my eighth try. I've never been very good with directions or numbers or time or names. Wide open spaces scare me.

But not so small pray you.

What a disappointment, that nobody knows best. It's just Goldilocks behind the curtain, eating up all the food and batting her eyelashes. The old guard forcibly displaced by a brunette with pale lips and the only way home.

Had they only known.

It's never too late to get lost and make a fool of oneself. Better than a lot of things.

My Car

Once I saw a drawing from a little kid, with writing that said that being a human is really just being an angel who came to Earth to try on a human suit for a little while. I never forgot this, and suspect that kids know a lot more than adults about these kinds of things.

My neighbor Nicole sold me my car about six years ago. It's seen a lot of life since then.

Nicole is an opposite kind human being from me. She's immaculate, steadfast, organized, polite and proper. Just so.

I'm sloppy, disorganized, inadvertently rude, often thoughtless, as wayward as the west wind.

When she sold me her 2001 Toyota Camry, it was in perfect shape. There was not a scratch or scrape to be seen. The papers for every repair and oil change were collected in a manila envelope in the glove compartment. We didn't know each other all that well, but she must have known enough from my mismatched socks and never-brushed hair to have a worried look on her face when we made the transaction. Keys in hand,

MY CAR

brow furrowed she asked "Now you will take care of it, won't you?"

I think deep down we both knew I was lying when I said "yes".

My car is the only place in the world that is mine, so of course it suffers. Despite my best intentions, trash and mugs and takeout containers pile up around me. Only when the trash is up to my knees do I clean it.

I always feel so good when I do, like I've got a fresh start. I swear I'll never let it get trashy again, as I've done a million times before.

I get into accidents.

Let me clarify. I get into accidents when I'm anxious, which is most of the time.

I smashed my hood in a few years ago. The road was slick that day and I was late to work and I slid five feet into the bumper in front of me. Now the hood is held down by duct tape.

Children point when I drive down the road. Their mothers tell them it's rude to point, then push them further back onto the sidewalk out of hitting range.

One day, after several hits to my driver's side, the window stopped working.

Another day the outside driver's side handle snapped off into my hand.

A few weeks later the inside handle also snapped off.

Now I have to crawl out my passenger side every time I get out. I used to try to park far enough away from places that nobody I know sees me. It sets a poor precedent to be emerging from the passenger side with trash falling out around my feet.

The car smells like wet. And old. And the various things I've imbibed in it.

I try to put my best face forward, pretending I'm not hanging on by a thread.

Still, I feel as broken as that car.

I'm constantly searching for ways to fill The Big Hole.

I lose things, break things, forget things, am easily overwhelmed. I have a bad back and a blood disease and autoimmune disorders and no matter how much I do or learn or accomplish on paper I feel like a little kid who is about to get in trouble.

If there is a God, and if our souls are really angels that come down from heaven to try on these human suits, I just know that my angel soul was tapping their toes impatiently waiting for the keys to this skin-suit when God walked up with a worried look and a furrowed brow and asked "Now you will take care of it, won't you?"

Deep down we probably both knew I was lying when I said "yes".

Tomato Porn

How I'm
  Trying to keep myself dry
  To keep myself wet

I hate sitting under the sun a bulging bulbous clown nose full to bursting you'd never know what's happening inside sitting pretty on a cool green vine why can't I be a cool green vine?

Every day the same question.

Do I split before my time and just keep oozing until I'm dry?

Or do I sit here throbbing bright red until someone puts their fingers around me, gentle and firm, plucks me swiftly from the vine I love, pierces my skin with their sharp white teeth until I run down their chin, slide under their tongue and squish past their gums there's just no delicate way to do this

…unless…

you've got a very sharp blade in your pocket, in which case you get to see how beautiful and messy I am on the inside before I fill your mouth up with a wreckage of seeds and juice and pulp and I wonder how is this so good?

Apples get such a bad wrap after the whole Eve debacle, but that's playboy stuff.

Tomatoes are smutty and messy and smell like heaven and dirt.

Shush, A Gift

I miss the mafia before they realized that it's better to make the law than break the law If you've got yourself some capital buy yourself a capitol hell we'll all be walking through fire even with the AC blasting that's the funny thing about Vegas you can get everything you want and nothing you need every moment is a gift but you forgot the 'argh' drop the A-G-H and you got yourself a grift made legit when the pirates own the ship.

Just drop the 'R' kiddo and nobody will get hurt.

Upside Down and In the Dark

Leaving tsunami zone
    But upside down

Typical

"I'll take care of you" I said and took your hand as we crossed into the tsunami zone.

We talked about what would happen if the earthquake came. You thought of all the ways we'd get stuck. The bottle necks and car crashes.

I said that we'd run and run until we were safe and that we'd be fine, all the while imagining that cartoon tidal wave taller than the Empire Building coming towards us in slow motion. You know the one. I tell you about it all the time because I've seen it a hundred times.

What I never tell you is that it's as real to me as you are. I can hold your warm hand, a little bit sweaty, and we're here, but also I see the wave in my peripheral.

I feel the car crash that ended that timeline way back when, and feel lucky to be here with you, even though I shouldn't be remembering things like that.

Eyes wide, you talked about your regrets. I hold them like I'm a cradle because even though sometimes I'm not here, I love you very much.

I can't hold myself but I think I can hold you and your Great sadness. I'm so very good at this part. I never had a choice.

You have to understand, I do the best I can, but I'm always running around on the strings, like a spider on ice skates. So far from home.

Always forgetting the wrong things and remembering the wrong things.

When we go back, it's dark out, so we don't even know when we cross over the tsunami zone.

A Dirty Dozen Plus One

And me with my messy hair, looking at what nature made without the benefit of an eighty dollar haircut LEAVE MY HAIR ALONE.

Just let me grow up through the cracks and expand wide, shatter and crack and become a hazard to mankind and a wonder to behold, or you know, a shriveled limping mess, make it to the good stuff and pay the price.

I don't want to be what you want me to be, I want to sing, and when all those lost women line up to tell me "it's not the choice I would have made but I like it" that's cool baby the choice we all would have made is overrated as a hot drink on a cold day in hell.

You be your bad self and I'll be my mad self and then you can stop trying to figure out what box to put me in sometimes slick as a sliding board sometimes a bale of hay in a hurricane.

I'm well over a dozen, more than half of them dirty, don't mind the prissy one she only shows up when the temperature is oppressive.

It won't be boring, I can tell you that much.

Leftovers

I ate the food you made me, too late, I know.
　It got cold.
　But I loved you with every bite,
Shivering and starving.
Thinking, 'Maybe this will save me'

She Caught a Draft

Behind me:

A staircase. It looks very short but is actually very long.

The red house that keeps showing up. Too red.

In front of me:

The mermaids.

Their song. The same song, the same wave that keeps showing up over and over while I sleep, ever since Nina left, and also before she came.

Between me and them:

The code word.

It's hard not to listen to the house, the staircase, the song, the wave. The cacophonous longing.

But the three letter word sits between us. That, and the voice of a friend who has known me a very long time.

Longer than that.

Even longer.

She says my name. A tether, it sticks.

Pesky. Pesky like the magic word, spoken the moment I was washed to shore, yellowed and apart at the seams.

Between them they pull me back from stepping through, even though the beautiful voices are singing my song, and honestly I wouldn't mind being held, even if their hands are cold and their fingers are sharp.

But I'm sorry. We've already discussed this.

A Jesus Guy

Sitting in the back of the record store it's a rainy night.
Can't tell the difference between disease and old age.
One you really should accept along with the honors.
One you fight the good fight.
Wait, that's not right.

I guess I'm here now, since it (all of it) stopped working and I stopped believing myself so I had no choice but to believe in myself instead.

Damn, I should have listened to the Buddha, but he was sitting there all smarmy and smiling in his robe, chubby and happy YOU CAN'T BE BOTH CHUBBY AND HAPPY EVERYBODY KNOWS THIS. Don't they?

I guess I'm a Jesus guy.
Flippin' tables to eternity. .
The key falls to the ground with a tinkle and it sounds like a dime,
but the face of it is worn away so we can only go on sound and Assumption.

A JESUS GUY

I know where I am in the pecking order anyway, [Born: FEMALE Skin: WHITE Class: MIDDLE] and that there's something to be said for it, but I got scum on my boots, slipped and fell and the doctors found a hairline fracture when I went into the machine.

The one that makes the scary noises and shows me what I look like on the inside.

You'd think the problem was about bringing slick boots into a clean kitchen, but I had just as much trouble with that false floor Mother put out.

All for me? All for *us*.

That was the year, the year *we* went out to hunt *our* own Christmas tree, guns cocked and locked, that I realized that I'm actually competent if the ground is solid and unmoving. If the wind would stop blowing.

Something I can lay my toes to.

But in this terrain?

Just give me a moment to get my bearings here, it's something unfortunately impossible to tell or teach, more a rant than a preach, you just have to get a feel for it.

Some people are just faster than others, depends on what? How slippery you are?

DOING OUR DAMNDEST

Not to be a martyr, but I'm grateful for that hairline fracture in this here head gasket.

At least it lets a little bit of light in.

That's not nothing.

Pink Blankets and Black Aprons

This morning I got to the cafe, put on my black apron, and started opening duties. I love my black apron. It helps me feel invisible, which some people wouldn't like, but I've found that it's better not to be noticed than to be noticed when you're trapped for eight hours in one place serving strangers.

As I was putting out our sign I saw a pink blanket in front of the neighboring empty storefront. Portland is sick with empty buildings and storefronts, the rents too high for businesses to make it long. The form under the blanket was ambiguous…it was impossible to tell their gender or their age.

I brought the pink blanket a croissant and a cup of coffee and silently placed it on the ground and saw five used needles scattered around it. I stood there for a few minutes to make sure the pink blanket was breathing.

It was.

So I stood there and contemplated the possible ramifications of giving a pink blanket around the corner a cup of coffee with our logo on it…I might be making more trouble for myself if pink blanket thinks that this cafe is safe place.

It's not.

If pink blanket thinks that there is a soft heart around I might be cleaning up needles or blood, or calling the police to break into the restroom again. I walk away, wishing on one hand that I could do more than a coffee and a croissant. And I tell myself that if a pink blanket comes in looking to use the restroom I'll just have to turn it away like I do anyone who isn't a paying customer.

No soft hearts here. Just pink blankets and black aprons.

Thing is

Thing is.
    Everything is fleeting. And you had to be there.

    The knotty parts are so real and everything else is just a screen dream.

Guilty. Give it a wooden hammer to hit home.
    Wood is hard not as hard as metal but pretty hard it leaves a mark.
    Don't go out. Stay in. Be safe.
    Oh yes though peoples is nice sometimes, we crawl out sometimes we tries we tries. We likes this, it wasn't so bad.

But let's stay inside it's cheaper and safer and comfortable.
    Less trouble.

Can't be a menace to society if you menacing the mirror. Smudges.
    We can make that work this isn't working I don't want to be Bothered, oh bother.
    Rustled.

It's okay. It's okay, practice feeling safe outside the bed outside the screen outside the cradle.

It's not perfect, this is practice, go out and get stronger with all that falling, magic doesn't work in a vacuum (really it doesn't I tried it's like a firefly).

She glows for such a short time and then it's gone, you have to go outside to feel her and let your eyes adjust to the dark. Otherwise it's just an electric picture.

You had to be there.
   You know?

We're doing the best we can.
   Aren't we?

Hanger

Hanging in there like that tooth that hung on for two weeks when I was eight.

By a thread of flesh.

Wiggling it like a bad habit.

Waggling it at people like a middle finger.

Grossing out the adults cause they can't handle that our skeletons are sometimes on the outside and once in a lifetime they all fall out.

Get it over with.

But not this one.

A Hanger.

Freaking everyone out.

Another Broken Mirror

I believed everything you ever told me but the one thing.

It was a lie but why would I cut that thread? I'm not a monster.
Just an interesting monster.

It's hard not to regret letting the margarine sit out to soften. Budget butter.
The cat got to it.

I told you so.

The flour unsifted sits to the side and out of sight. Unthought of. Not of bread or much else.

I told you so.

Everything after that day was begging on borrowed time anyway.
I never was one for walking away, but in forgetting I excelled.

Ever the exile.

ANOTHER BROKEN MIRROR

It's an easy A, to forget when there's a string tied to your shoe.

The unspoken bit…Survey says?

To your other shoe.
   Now I'm barefoot and bloody on the mirror I broke in one of my tempers.

There's a hole on the floor. I finally found it.
   A Tom and Jerry cartoon so predictable it's funny. And here I was staring at the ceiling.

Doing my best not to be loved because that's the most dangerous place in the whirled. Candy coated. We go every Sundae.

I'll do my best.

It's not much on paper, that I'll admit, but it's not nothing.

It's not an etiquette book written in invisible red ink.

It's not your fingerprint from when they took you away.

It's not a perfect lie perched precariously on stilts that go all the way up to the ceiling.

It's not the Maypole nor the April, March pole nor the North Pole nor any other straight and narrow thing.

It's not the eight pairs of crutches from all the spills I took. My skinny ankles, my heavy head.

Or maybe it is. Maybe it's exactly the same.

Mouth Breather

Today my energy is down again. So I'll ease the slow simmer of medical fatigue with some tap water words and a nap.

I have to add the 'medical' these days since just about everyone around me struggles with fatigue of other flavors.

A type of fatigue for every color of the rainbow.

And a reaction to our reflections for every color of the rainbow.

Compassion being quiet. Disgust being loud.

Also love and hate, patience and anger. Everything good and everything bad. Nothing in between.

And in every way we discount ourselves, we will eventually discount others.
　In every way we're trapped, we will eventually trap others.
　These sweet and sorry reflections.
　It's part of the Forgetting.

Remembering is too large for the overhead compartment. With all the contents shifting you'll want it stored somewhere else anyway.

Trust the baggage handlers and prepare for a bumpy ride.

I can usually sleep through the whole flight. Mouth open and catching my breath before we glide silently through the cloud cover.

Julio and the Ants

That wasn't the last time.

But.

The drugs aren't working the way they used to and I'm unwilling to dig another inch of this grave, so I'll protest by laying down in it. That makes sense doesn't it?

No need to worry the boys in black, it's gonna be a peaceful one.

Like one of them stories you like to tell.

A little switch just flipped. (Honestly. I'm relieved.)

It wasn't as fun as I hoped it would be though.

We have an island in our kitchen that the ants can't get to.
 They tried, my big human feet make me feel like a God, I can walk from the sink to the island, get it everything it needs, ant-free.

Drop a tomato on the island
Plop
Another glorious gift from god.

I had less trouble with learning new pronouns than I had with turning an "I" into a "we".
  A "my" into an "our"
  That drives the value up, just ask economists.

My kitchen has ants.
  Our kitchen has ants.
  The kitchen has ants.
  Your kitchen has ants.

The way I trip and stumble over the *our* tells you everything you need to know about the ship.

The ants are back, okay?

Can't stop the ants.

I think that particular tunnel lasted about two years, and when I came out the other side I was Changed.

I Hear Julio's voice in my head and it says "you would have changed anyway" and my mental projection of him shrugs.

That Perfect Love shrug.

The Ice Queen

Jack and Stacey come into the cafe every day. Sometimes twice a day.

They are an older couple with lots of money. I don't know how they got their money, but they hold onto it and grow it by working the system in every way they can.

Every year they manage a free thirty day trip to Europe with these deals. Stacey explained to me, "We don't need to do this… it's a hobby", as they walk away from the empty tip jar, all smiles. The very picture of grace.

Never in my years at the cafe have they put money in the tip jar. I would be a dirty liar if I didn't admit that regulars who don't tip have a different experience than regulars who tip.

The wealthy non-tippers don't have a bad experience, but they wonder why these people who they feel should be their friends, or at least chummy, don't open up to them. They see us interacting with other customers and note the difference. They expect our friendship and our service, on their terms.

We are all as nice as we have to be to these people, but they don't get jokes, they don't get the unexpected thirty minute discussions, and they don't get the kind of warmth that we save for people who have shown that they see the work we're doing.

And before you balk, I'll tell you right off the bat, It's not about the amount of money someone leaves. A few coins in the tip jar shows that the work we are doing is valued.

I'm not sure if it's their policy not to tip at all, or not to tip on coffee, but all the employees have a reticent relationship with them due to this. Maybe that's why they have unkind nicknames for all of the baristas in the cafe. Denigrating nicknames that reveal the lens through which they view us.

They call me The Ice Queen.

This particular morning Jack and Stacey had just returned from one of their trips.

Their friend Tom came in and they all sat together, comparing their many experiences in Italy. While they softly talked, a black man about my age with a face tattoo walked in. He seemed like he was a little out of it, and apologetic.

He asked me if I could break a $20 for the bus, because he was on his way to rehab. I reluctantly broke his twenty, and we chatted, or more accurately, he talked at me until my guard dropped halfway.

Yeah, he seemed pretty high, but he wasn't totally gone. He told me his name was Marqueez, and that he was headed to rehab because he was broke again.

He told me "I'm ready this time, I'm ready this time. I'm doing this for my boy. He's so smart. He's gonna be the first man in the family to go to college. He's smarter than me, but I'm going to make him proud. I'm ready this time".

By this point, he'd won me over, a fellow addict, a perpetual loser; but Marqueez stayed a little longer than I would have liked, with work to do and no money being exchanged. He was nervous to get on the bus I could tell, but he could also tell that I was ready for him to leave. A non-customer. He said as much.

I heard Stacey, Jack, and Tom talking about the gelato in Sicily. The best in the world. I heard Marqueez still talking to me, apologizing for nothing in particular, just for being. He looked at me and his eyes were wet and my focus snapped back to him. He said "Thank you. I'm gonna come back when I'm clean and I'm gonna get some coffee from you". He walked over to the tip jar and dropped in a quarter.

In a rare moment I said "Marqueez, come back when you're out and your coffee is free". He was tugging at my heart strings. Maybe I was a sucker; maybe he knew he'd found himself a barista who considered herself a Grade A fuck up.

I sized up my company in the cafe and realized I preferred him to the world travelers. I hoped Marqueez came back and I told him so. I leaned towards him and quietly told him "I've had troubles with drugs and alcohol too, most of my life. If you want to get clean, I know you can do it". I spoke softly enough so that the world travelers couldn't hear me share this information about myself. I knew enough then not to bleed in the water when sharks are around.

He reached across the bar with his hands out and I hesitated, not loving touch at work, or ever; but against my better judgement I took his dry hands in my dry hands. His were cracked and calloused against my own coffee-stained fingers. We just stood there with our hearts beating in our chests, thinking our own thoughts, looking into each other's eyes. Without another word he left. I was relieved that the intimate and intense moment was over, and that the interaction hadn't turned sour in some way.

Jack and Stacey finished their coffee and came over to me and suggested that I get some carpeting for the cafe. "Starbucks is doing that you know, they have these little cozy nooks to curl up in. You should think about it. It's a good idea. Makes it feel like a living room". I gave them my coldest, most regal smile and poured some bleach into my mop bucket.

I could have put on more of a show for them, pretend that I was giving their suggestion a fair shot and that I'd run it to corporate, but I wouldn't want to disappoint them.

After all, I Am the Ice Queen.

you paid for it

You can plan for every little scenario.

Every eventuality.

You can practice, and watch, and quietly learn, and fall and get back up.

Take the criticism.

You can push yourself past what you thought your limits were and listen to your heart.

You can try to be nice and you can try to be hard.

And sometimes you still have a little cat vomit on your shoe.

That's life, man.

Wipe it off.

Come back tomorrow.

With even less cat vomit on your shoe.

Or. Even. *More*.

Story Witch

Two bit

Tin type

    Steaming where the rains hits

If it fits I sits

Behind the storm cloud

A little blue in my gold

or a little gold in my blue

3 or so months seems like a good round number

I never was one for remembering or marking dates

Almost like it was made up

To make sense
  Of the insensible

DOING OUR DAMNDEST

Of all of things I thought I could never live without

But here I am

Not remembering your birthday again

Only knowing the swells and the ebbs and the way things go

Only knowing how to spin a yarn

Confident only in that casting on and casting off are the hardest parts.

Remind me

The Bunker

I got a bunker set aside. For the end of the world.

It's in a place they'll never find, not until they plug my head into the machines we were supposed to be raging against, not until they kill the light, which we were also supposed to be raging against.

Ahem

The universe is unknowable and my head is unknoweringable, and it's all good, until space trash starts colliding with a perfectly planned mission, then it's all just shooting stars.

Which is what I figured when I was 8 years old anyway, when I found out that there's no such thing as fair and there's no such thing as safe, so what the hell?

Tweedledee and Tweedledum make more sense than this. Yes yes yes, we're all mad hare.

The kingdom for a hat full of mercury. For a sweet dip in a kiddie size Kool Aid pool.

The safest place I've ever been was in a hospital bed, most of my blood digested and disposed without a pink slip or verbal notice or nothing.

Which brings me back to this bunker.

Splits and Splones

So many entertainers masquerading as authorities.
The ability to excite the imagination of a nation made numb and dumb by our self defeating worship of convenience went sideways now it's a joke except for the wholesale slaughter coming soon to a theater near you threatened by words lending power to deeds when the whole castle is built on a mole hill pumped and dumped throbbing with dopa and sero and the oxy and the means and the tins and the sins don't even talk to me about it I'm the one who's been making a spectacle of themself theirself themself wearing addiction on my sleeve since I finally looked in the mirror talking to everyone about it until she says "you know you're not special everyone struggles with it" which is a real bummer because every day hurts and it helps to think oneself madperson on the street screaming into the sky THE END IS NIGH but all that noise isn't coming from mouths its coming from the screens and where once the screams turned to songs now it's just a load of space trash which eill be shooting stars eventually anyway.

Earmuffs children there's only so many ear hairs to split before you find yourself deaf and dumb.

Nor Nary

The only perfect beasts are the ones covered in soft fur. Unknowingly so.

The things I lost I can barely remember.

Everything always remains the same. The darkness has always been there, waiting to be noticed. It becomes me. And sometimes in a dream I can see that the light does too.

But the sameness of it all.

The space between my eyes still hurts.

I still don't understand where I end and you begin.

I still want what is, now I can see it clearly, not for me.

If only I could get clean. No no I mean like really clean. To unbecome with nary a care-y. Nary a squeak nor nary a squawk.

Nor Nary Nor Nary Nor Nary.

NOR NARY

I guess we're just about half past noon, even if the odds are stacked for an early bedtime and my toes are crossed for a little snack.

I'd like to drift off with a full belly and cute little crumbs around my mouth that talked so much and said so little.

Something in Common

He asks me if it's hard being sober.

I tell him no. It's not hard.

>Of course, I'd be lying if I said I didn't think about it.
I think about drugs and alcohol when I'm having a difficult time.
When I'm stressed.
Or angry.
Or sad.

That's when I wish I had something to take the edge off.

But no, it's not hard.
It's easy.

I won't lie, I do think about drugs and alcohol when I'm happy.
When I'm on vacation,
or looking at stars,
or playing music,
or connecting with someone.

That's when I wish I had something to make it feel even better.

But being sober is the easiest thing in the world. You just don't take drugs or drink alcohol anymore.

Sure, I think about drugs and alcohol on rainy days.
   And beautiful crisp fall days
   and snow days,
   and hot summer days,
   and nights.

Yes, I think about it when I have to work a lot,
   and when I take time off work.

I think about it when I'm alone
   and also when I'm with people.

I think about it when I'm feeling sorry for myself
   and when I'm being strong.

But no, it's not really so hard being sober.

It's the being that's hard.

Hard Boiled Afternoon

I'm standing at the cafe I work at, drawing faces on the eggs and smiling to myself. Angry Egg. Sad Egg. Happy Egg. Surprised Egg. Steph Egg.

It's a stupid way to amuse myself and break up the monotony. I've been feeling off lately.

Sad Egg.

I've been stuck in a negative place in my head where everyone is semi out to get me and my life is going nowhere and pretty much over at 36. Two weeks ago I stopped taking 5-htp, the natural antidepressant I'd been on for years. I attribute my dark mood to that, and dismiss it best I can. I used to fight the waves of mood swings that take me, now I just ride them out and try not to break anything along the way.

Complacent Egg.

A woman walks in with a brown skirt and a fitted plaid shirt, her pretty brown hair just so. She approaches me as a scientist would approach a drugged Panther. Carefully, but with a mission.

Determined Egg.

She looks at me, smiles, and starts to ask for something but stops herself, putting her hands in the air as if to placate me.

So far, I've said nothing.
"How are you?" she asks.

I smile. "I'm well, how are you?"

Five years ago lying would have bothered me. If I wasn't doing well I would say something innocuous like "Oh, I'm fair to middlin". Now I'd rather expedite the interaction.

"Good. Okay. So. I'd like a breakfast sandwich with an egg BUT can I get it without the skin?"

I look at her and wait, confused but not wanting to ask her what she means.
   She tells me anyway.

"You know how baked egg gets a skin? Well I want the egg well done, but that skin is just Yuck right? Do you mind making sure there's no skin on it?"
   I feel my mind standing at a crossroads. I'm trying to be more positive so I decide not to be a dick. I smile at her and say "You sure you don't want me to leave it on? A thick skin sure could come in handy these days."

Laughing Egg.

She looks at me, not understanding my joke, trying to hide her annoyance, waiting for me to acknowledge that I understand her.

Angry Egg.

I tell her the price without any sign that I heard her or understand her request.

Worried Egg.

I walk over to the food prep area and find the Steph Egg. I crack it open into the little frying pan, smiling to myself. I make sounds effects under my breath of a plane crashing and burning and the pale yellow insides slide into the pan, yolk breaking right away. You always know when you've gotten eggs from a caged chicken. Weak shell weak yolk.

She sits down and nervously stares at me and I ignore her silent anxiety, watching the egg harden in the pan with morbid delight.

When it's done I slide it out and find this skin she's talking about…something I've never thought about in my time on this planet.

Surprised Egg.

I call out the sandwich and she examines it right there and audibly sighs in relief, then gingerly places a dollar in the tip jar, as if I didn't know all about my good friend Pavlov and his dogs.

I sweep the shell of the Steph Egg in the trash can and watch her take the first bite out of the corner of my eye.

I think about making a post about Egg Skin Lady. My cafe posts always pop off. But I don't feel funny right now so fuck it. Fuck the algorithm. People shouldn't always get what they want.

People want selfies and Spotify and free shipping and their food containers to say Organic. Giving people exactly what they want isn't all it's cracked up to be. (Cracked up. Get it?)

Another customer walks in and I tell them I'll be right with them. They smile and say "take your time".

As I quickly finish cleaning up the station that will get dirty and clean again dozens of times before the end of my shift, I think of all the things I could say to them about my time.

My Time.

Instead I walk over and give her a perfunctory smile and say "What can I get for you"

Tired Egg

Pavlov's Bitches

"We're all Pavlov's bitches" I say with a self satisfied smile.

He grimaces in distaste. "You don't need to be so hard all the time." he says. "Softer. You must be softer."

Outwardly, I am chastised.

I know, I know. I know better than to let it show. Nobody likes a bitter woman. A bitter anyone.

Manifest your destiny. Positive thinking. Let it roll off your back. Practice gratitude. That's the power of love.

"I know I know" I say. And isn't that convenient, all of us Pavlov's BITCHES. (yeah take that)

None of us Bukowski's sluts.

Never doing it for free because we love it, kitten heels clicking across a field of bones.

I've gotten pretty good at walking on these things.

Broken Edges

In the same whiskey-laden breath he admits that he can't believe we're talking. He's thought about this so many times. Do I want him to come over?

No. I don't.

He texted me and asked if I could talk. He was relapsing. A man who I met at work who caught me in an emotional moment and asked me if I was okay.

It came out quickly, as it so often does, that we were both drug and alcohol recovery, struggling with sobriety. We chatted over the course of a year at work, over the counter, quickly updating each other on sobriety or lack thereof.

The easy intimacy of two addicts, creating another tenuous connection that might just be the one that keeps one of us from spinning off into the universe one random evening.

I tell him that staying on the phone is exactly the support I'm willing to give him and no more. I'm not a sponsor.

He says "Of course", then some switch flips and he says "You're obsessed with yourself. Your ego is massive."

I'm speechless. He laughs, dumbly, cruelly, drunk and horny.

This was a mistake.

I'm troubled after the conversation so I ask myself my favorite helpful question, what did I learn? The answer is nothing.

No wait, I should be more guarded. No wait, I'm plenty guarded. No wait, I'm guarded with the wrong people. No wait, why would I agree to talk to a drunk stranger on the phone?

Heavy and sad and stupid. Something is trying to tell me something but my head is tied to my body, a balloon to a string and I don't know what's going on. I can't sift through the wrongness to find the rightness.

He's right. He must have smelled it on me. I secretly knew I was the worst. Check out this ego on the world's worst person.

A truth. Nothing is sacred, especially not the sharp edges of broken glass on the bar room floor.

And here I've been tiptoeing around like a blue ballerina. A Faberge egg. Hard Boiled.

Even Then

So many years ago I made a decision, that I was not to be trusted. That my brain was a weak and traitorous, slanderous series of impulses, pursuing escape from pain and stalking pleasure at any cost all costs every last scent.

And for a long time that helped me. Until eventually I needed it less and less, the constant reminder that I'm a traveling circus, a conglomeration of sad once-wild beasts in too-small cages being gawked at by people paying too little. Insufficient funds.

These days though, I find I need it more and more.

Don't trust the circus. A silent prayer.

The ribcages and lethargy will just make you sad. More dangerous than anything roaming free, waiting for you to let your guard down.

Look away at the stories that the clouds tell. It's a better place, with better tails.

I tell myself.

EVEN THEN

These days I have to wait until I'm rested and fed and counted to ten before I turn to them, with an uneasy heart. With enough strength to not stretch my fingers through their cages and scratch behind their scabby ears.

Even then…

A True Agnostic

Times are tough for a true agnostic.

I wander around the house muttering under my breath, tasting smoke residue on my lips.

Raised Catholic, I go through the motions, crossing myself, in the name of the Father, the Son, and the Holy Spirit.

Dear God, It's me Stephanie…He's got to be getting tired of that joke.
 I negotiate, wheedle, plea.

I wander into the bathroom and look into the mirror, covered in condensation from the water I've been boiling nonstop for the last three days. I read online that it reduces wildfire smoke and I try everything I read online. Call it faith.

I wipe my hand over the fog and see my reflection speckled with flecks. I looked tired and older, and I don't really care.

Dear God make it rain so that the wildfires slow down.

A TRUE AGNOSTIC

It was a weak prayer and I know it.

Maybe it'll join up with all the true Christians' prayers and give it the push it needs. Up through the smoke, the clouds, higher, through the pearly gates, up the big hill, into God's mansion, past his office door, to land in front of his face on his big wooden desk. Please sir, push this one through. I promise I'll be a better person.

I wander aimlessly to the kitchen. The water is almost boiled down. I add more and look at the four leaf clovers I have been drying all year. I open the jar and dump them into the hot water and say "Witchcraft" out loud.

A spell like a prayer.

I throw in some dried cherry blossoms and watch them bloom and dance in the water. They are transparent now, like jellyfish...even more delicate than when they first fell. Kamikaze Ballerina Ghosts.

I remember sitting on my porch and watching them bloom. When it was spring.

I walk to the bedroom and talk to my grandmother's picture. I ask her what she would have thought of all of this, and tell her that I wish she was here and that I'm glad she's not here for this.

I light a candle for Linda and try to recall what it felt like when she held me in her arms in her hospital room. Instead my mind flashes to the next day, when we snuck her out of the hospital in her gown so she could smoke some weed and feel the grass on her feet and how she turned her face to the sun and wept because she missed dancing and I sang her her song…

loving life so much that it hurt, as it was slipping through her fingers.

I run a bath, hoping it will clear my headache. I sink into water that burns my skin and turns it bright pink.

Water-burning skin is a feeling. It's a concrete feeling, not like smoke particles seeping into your lungs like a slow pillow to the face.

I'll always have my books. Except I can't concentrate and I let it fall to the floor outside the tub.

My cat walks up to me and I offer her my wet fingers to lick. She does, and starts purring. She loves licking bathwater off my fingers. Gross little cat.

Then she settles into a perfect fuzzy ball right next to me, close enough for me to hear her purring.

In the next room, my partner shuffles papers and I know my little family is close enough to touch.

Nothing else matters. For right now.

Entertaining Thoughts

Last night after work I went for a long night walk and decided to veer into a dingy little bar near my house I'd never been to.

It was perfect in every way. This was the kind of bar I'd be frequenting a few times a week if I still drank.

There were four poker machines, three pinballs, two pool tables, and one Karaoke DJ. Small but not too small, dirty, but not too dirty. I don't avoid bars or places where people drink, but I usually don't choose to spend much time at them either. It felt like good to be there. Kind of like coming home. More so than the dingy meeting rooms of AA and NA meetings.

It was early in the night. Karaoke had just started. I wanted to do some karaoke, which was rare for me. I wanted to talk to strangers. There was a young man behind me who was a likely candidate but seemed like he needed more liquid courage before having a conversation with a stranger.

I kept eyeballing his drink. A Maker's Mark with way too much ice for my taste. It was a mound of small chips and the amber liquid was lightening too quickly. He didn't seem to mind.

I was uncharacteristically hootin' and hollerin' for each performer, singing along with songs over my soda water with bitters and lime, remembering how fun I used to be. (Sobriety and aging have some confusing parallels).

There was a lot of passive resistance when I quit drinking. Questions posed, such as, 'Do you think you'll ever have a drink again?' 'We used to have so much fun' and comments like 'It's good to take a break sometimes' or 'You're not really an alcoholic' or 'You never seemed like you had problem to me'.

That's because I rarely made a scene when I was drinking. I was usually a happy drunk, pretty light and easy. When I hit black out drunk I was told that I sat quietly giggling to myself. At the bar I'd start with a double tall whiskey soda. Throughout the night I'd order one to four more depending on where I was at in my alcoholism. Towards the end it'd be four double tall whiskey sodas and a quick shot right before I left the bar when nobody but the bartender was looking.

Then I'd go home and pick up a six pack of cider or a bottle of wine, polish that off, and then ransack whatever was in the house.

Other days, I'd get a fifth and drink it alone, usually getting two thirds of the way through it…just enough left to start early the next day.

Like an iceberg, the part of my alcohol abuse that people could see was not the half of it. I wasn't like some of my friends, whose problems were evident. On the occasion that I got too drunk in front of people, I regretted it. My clueless friends would laugh and recount to me how wasted I had been. They didn't know how much it hurt and shamed me to hear about how I had fallen down a flight of stairs or passed out on the lawn.

I didn't talk about the chipped tailbone, the bruises, the sprained wrist, or how I spent every morning trying to piece together what I had done based on running my hands over my body for injuries and soreness, like a twisted Sherlock Holmes.

I didn't talk about the trips to Planned Parenthood, trying to explain to the doctor that I wasn't sure if I'd had unprotected intercourse or if I'd even had intercourse.

But that's old news. That was four years ago. A lifetime.

These days I consider….loopholes. Half jokingly, half wishfully. The airport is a loophole. A Christmas alone. Accidentally being served a drink with alcohol. And my favorite:

Bum Da Da Bum!

The Apocalypse.

As fine a time to drink as any.

I'd quietly planned on drinking again before I die. Maybe it's the news and the internet spinning every disaster, but it sure does feel like we're smack dab in the middle of Shit Creek, doesn't it?

I finished my soda water and almost unconsciously noted the bar as a great possibility for a relapse location, knowing I was nowhere near being able to handle a drink, not with exciting daydreams of the Relapocalypse dancing in my head.

I walked home and didn't think too hard on my night, but thoughts ran over my brain like water and flowed away:
   Why don't we ever hear from the people who were sober for a long time and then started drinking responsibly? I know they're out there. I met one. Once.

And what would really be the issue with drinking once or twice a year…would I be out of the club if I did that?

People can change….can't people change? Sure, I exhibit addict tendencies every day that trouble me and take up a ton of my mental resources, but it's been so long since I drank… maybe that's not the problem anymore.

Maybe I'm smarter and more responsible now.

I watched the thoughts come and go. Thoughts are just thoughts. They can't hurt you if you don't entertain them. At least that's what I'd been told.

That night I had a relapse dream. I have them a few times a year.

ENTERTAINING THOUGHTS

I was getting ready for a show and my sister and a friend were there. It was mostly me sneaking off the the bathroom to pour myself a glass of red wine over a mound of ice. When my friend knocked on the door I quickly hid the glass under the sink, then when she closed the door behind her I chugged her glass of un-iced red wine in one gulp. Neither my sister nor my friend suspected anything, and that's where the dream ended.

I woke up, feeling a little off and little guilty.

Goodness. Brains. They do have a way of making themselves heard.

In today's news, Trump suggested nuking hurricanes to stop them and the Amazon fires continue to burn. Sure does feel like world is ending, but we're not there yet.

I suspect that humanity really screwed the pooch on this chapter of life on Earth, but I also think that just because we can finally see what we're doing, doesn't mean we're all that close.

So it looks like one of my favorite loophole scenarios will have to wait.

Maybe tomorrow.

One day at a time and all that.

(This piece was hilariously written towards the end of 2019. If James Earl Jones were narrating this it would end with: "That day would come sooner than she thought")

Things That Happen

Such the magician that she chose her labyrinth above all else.

And when she poked her head out

from her dizzy hole

she found her face

had changed.

A Flight

In Colon, Michigan (yes, Colon) there is a graveyard of magicians. The setup keeps running through my head "a graveyard of magicians walk into a bar".

I don't know the punchline yet, but if I know anything about magicians it will come to me when I'm about to get kicked in the teeth.

Instead I hear his voice, the reflection. "Everybody needs to take a break from the pub sometimes" followed by "sorry, did you want a cold one?"

No, no thank you magician, my mirror.

Gosh all on your own there you looked sad for a moment. But the lot of you is a spectacle.

A spectacle of magicians.

And in that place, more mirrors. Grandiose and lower to the ground.

The magnificent fraud.

You can call me Great.

We mostly get to choose our names, that much is true. But how they will see us, it is what it is.

I'm glad for them. To meet them here.

The well-intentioned weavers, masters of prestidigitation and pomp.

I got to choose my name, but how they will see me, that is what it is.

Everything dissolves into the smoke, snuggled tight against mirrors.

A flight of magicians.

Just like me.

It Ain't Easy Being Prey

The little birds fly away when I go outside.

"Good for them" I think to myself.

Me, I'm one of Harlow's monkeys, left to be interrogated in a dark room with a bright ass light in my face. A dark room in the middle of a building in the middle of a complex where everything looks the same. What would you even do if you got out?

Nah, better to play along, it's a game. You can sit there sulking and maybe they'll bring you a Mountain Dew. It's climate controlled, and sometimes they let you rest.

And that's when you can concentrate and dream about being a little bird.

Too small to notice, too quick to catch.

Sushi For Your Thought?

You'll always know how beautiful
    Or not beautiful he finds you.

    He lets you know.

You're a fish in a bowl.

Either way
    The male gaze gets you.

Fins pinned for curious observation
    Or awed at how confident you are for someone who rates so low on the picture show.
    A question never asked.

They marvel at a pretty one, until it's clear,
    her disinterest in being poke-d.

Then the bitter side eye.
    THIS bitch.

Men are always decent until you've said yes or no, then you're

just once or future property.
  A thin red line to cross before thee becomes thine.

The scars become her.
  At least I think so.
  And I tell her.
  Maybe it's not worth much from a fellow fish with a yellow tail,
  Sushi grade coward like me.

But I've got this way with words.
  Sharp knives that tell no lies.

And I said that men are always decent until you've said yes or no.

The earth is shaking.

Red

Under your skin lies the you you used to be
    A U-Haul of too tall tales
    A collection of fictional stories loosely based on true events
   That made you into the barbed hook
   That the fat lady sings and swings from

Which just goes to show you that a little blood goes a long way and lot of blood goes nowhere at all
   Until it spills on the carpet
   The red I loved so much
   The lies I used to be
   Stay little, Red, and keep riding

It doesn't have to be perfect, I can see the old you through the new stripes you took forever to choose.

It wasn't the pattern. It wasn't the hook. Just give me a cool wall for me to rest my cheek on when I grow tired.

And me, in my red house with my red walls and just a hint of yellow madness peeking past the peeling paint.

Just another story I told myself to pass the time, a gnat in the molasses of Seattle rush hour with a little time to kill and poetry oozing from my thorn bites.

Demetria's Sweaters

Demetria is the sternest, coldest old bat you've ever met.

The private school I teach at operates out of a church that rents its space to different programs, so there's plenty of coordinating with all kinds of people with different reasons for being there.

She has never been particularly nice, and this little church is her kingdom…the only place in this world where she has any control.

I've known a few people who worked under her, and they don't have nice things to say. Mostly they have learned how to dance around her and suggest I do the same.

For some reason I don't dislike Demetria. I don't know, I guess I feel like she's earned her right to not smile and be particularly nice to people. I hope I'm happier when I'm her age, but if not, I want to be grumpy without getting hassled about it.

After years at the cafe, I learned the fine art of killing them with kindness, and I've been dusting off my skills with Demetria. She was surprised when I continued to greet her every day with a bright smile, shining my too-bright light on her, regardless of her response or lack thereof.

Then a core staff member took a leave, and suddenly I was Demetria's go-to receiver of complaints.

It's interesting, to watch someone work to try to be calm and patient and pleasant, when they are none of these things. Instead she comes off as condescending, like she's talking to someone stupid. And that's okay. My customer service routine can also be condescending, particularly in the face of someone determinedly prickly.

Demetria has demonstrated to me her preternatural ability to block off pathways without seeming to do it on purpose. It's like playing slow-motion basketball, she can pivot her body in such a way to cut off all pathways to one's destination. (See Terminator 2: Villian.)

I can see Demetria trying to be more important to the church, trying to help things run, trying to be seen and heard…instead Demetria got herself kicked out of the church office by the other staff members, who decided life is too short and pay is too little to deal with her.

She created a makeshift desk in the hallway with a container of pens labeled "Demetria's Pens Do Not Use".

The only thing that is blessedly out of character for Demetria is her Christmas sweaters. She wears the most garish Christmas sweaters, with brilliant reds and greens; Santa Claus and Jesus co-exist comfortably on her wardrobe. She wears a different sweater every day of December, and will engage in pleasant conversation about them if prompted.

I guess I like Demetria. She, like most of my relationships at the school, is best taken in small bites, with lightness and humor.

I understand that she can be mean. I understand that she can be a tiny tyrant. I never want to be cornered by her if I can help it.

And yet, she represents something important to me.

We don't get to choose much in this life. We sometimes get to choose how we leave, and sometimes we get to choose how we respond and rebound. Demetria has chosen to respond negatively to most things. No rebound.

But damn it, it's *some*thing. She comes to work every day. She cantankerously doles out free lunches to the homeless. Demetria is here.

Out in the hallway.

In her Christmas sweaters.

With her container of untouchable pens.

Losers

I love being around them.

Grains of stardust that look like any old dust and it's not until they gather that you really see them shine.

The hungry and the thirsty and the lost and the extraterrestrial and the neurodivergent and the wounded and the builders.

The ones that fell on their faces over and over and over and got up over and over and over.

Finding childish glee in what they can.

Puffed up chest rolling into a room hunched over and filled with shame for taking any oxygen at all stains on their shirts threadbare and frayed.

The ones who always save you a spot at the table, no matter how wretched and sorry you might be no matter that you bit the hand that fed you no matter that you looked at them and took them for everyday dust.

They understand mistakes.

The pornographic cartoon mermaid the grown ass woman in cat ears the old man with noise canceling headphones the leprechaun with one lens missing from his sunglasses the man who mistook his 70's couch for a blazer.

The never-no-haircuts club the barefoot betties.

I can breathe here. I feel shiny here.

No longer just a speck of dust in my room alone building worlds evil and great in my head. World that will bloom and wither before someone has a chance to stumble by and say "hey that's cool".

Not a winner in the bunch. No plans for the future. The rungs of their ignored ladders are piled up in the corner ready to feed the fire.

I'm so tired of trying to do stuff the right way. The rules keep changing and the fine lines around my eyes sit tight in their pockets where my wondering eyes leave my hard drive full and my lips speechless.

Gimme the gutter, Oscar.

I hear the view of the stars can't be beat. All around me too.

Cakes for the Lady

I gave it an honest go, to make myself smaller. Hunched and bunched and spoke softly and not at all. Got real skinny and all the while my beautiful iced cakes went to the angry lady in the back room with the red welts and the dirty feet. She just kept slamming her face into them and went for the jugular, didn't even have a taste. A waste. Terrifying. Better to fill the house up knock over a few vases and move out to where the stars are only small because they're so far away. I thought I'd be lonely out here but no more than before, and it's nice to watch the shadow of my wings on the ground in the morning. Fearsome and full of potential between that first cup of coffee and a nap.

Masks at my feet. Just for fun.

Cowboy Stuff

What an absurd and heartbreaking world that stands behind us with a self-satisfied grin and a stick poking into our ribs, with a half whispered "put em up pardner".

Still and Always wide-eyed with wonder, from the dirt I'll be buried in to the clouds where my head resides, heart pounding in my ears and my chest and my temples the back of my knees and the soles of my feet, I do as they say and I put 'em up.

Weighing my options: Surrender with great shame or make a run for it. Escape, lost but free.

And if I get shot in the back? I'll make a hell of a show of it, body flying chest forward wings spread eyes staring, freed from their burden of seeing.

Shall we do our damndest?

Yes, Let's.

Spring loaded and zig-zagging for the trees, dinner bell nipping at my heels, I'll pretend I can't hear it, consequences be damned.

Because there's nothing more important than this, this breathless powerful tricky joyful being, fulfilling every promise.

An intermittent God with a real forgetting problem.

Oh gimme a break. I know heresy, and that ain't it.

I ain't afraid of God. The only thing I dread is the dinner bell, and once I'm all washed up, even that's not so bad.

Surrounded by faces that haven't been seen since morning, where the only thing broken is bread.

Promises, promises.

But for now you've got a stick in your rib, a decision to make, and not much time to make it.

Shall we then?

Rogue Agent

Agent Strange, reporting for duty.

I trust the details of my mission will be made clear to me in time. For now I continue to stay vigilant for messages, and hope that I'm not being led astray.

Yesterday, a hawk flew directly into my eye-line and the lady on the wall whispered in tones too hushed to decipher.

It sounded like a song. It was familiar to me somehow.

Grandmother's pearls turned up and with it her secret locket with a picture of the younger me.

The one who recorded her voice onto a cassette tape and tried to share with me a secret, cut off by a Spice Girls song on a mixed tape I was making for a friend.

I never got her full message, but I remember recording it in my grandmother's row home in Philadelphia after a dinner of canned beans and boiled hot dogs.

She was about to tell me the secret to happiness.

Always with the jokes.

UV Gone Mad

I don't understand you sunny weather people.

Don't get me wrong, I can enjoy a cool spring breeze on a warm day as much as the next guy, but to seek out the sun until your skin tingles with delight? Enough with the Vitamin D already.

The only time I can sit still without running my mind on high is during a storm.

Let's listen for the thunder and bate our breath for the lightning. Let the heavy rains fill our ear drums and wash away the melancholies. Let the ever changing gradations of blue and grey secret pinks and purples fill up our eye sockets and drive out the every day horrors.

There was that time I went out in the hurricane. I didn't tell anyone where I was going and I went to the shoreline and stood next to the her, arms spread wide, leaning forward into wind, sand biting my face and arms. Heart strapped to the end of kite with a key dangling, waiting for a kiss from the Gods.

UV GONE MAD

Mind quiet and still.

I just don't know about you *sunny weather people*. Baking like chickens. Frickin Icarus.

No, no, I know, I know. The seasonal depression people breathing a sigh of relief when the clouds part.

You enjoy your light spring breezes. I'll enjoy my hurricane force winds.

We'll meet somewhere in the middle for a cup of tea and something sweet.

Something we can all agree on.

DOING OUR DAMNDEST

32 Seconds with Jack

At the school I work at, a nonprofit arts school for adults with intellectual and developmental disabilities, there's a student named Jack.

I've only ever seen Jack online.

He looks like he's in his 20's, has blonde hair, and wears his grin like a uniform. Mouth stretched in a perpetual smile, his eyes slide first to the left, then to the right.

When answering questions, Jack always repeats the question first, like he's asking you the question right back.

"Are you coming to the Halloween Dance?" I ask.

Grin fixed, his eyes swing wide, left, then right.

"Am I coming to the Halloween dance"

Seconds pass, tick tock tick tock...

"Yes, I'm coming to the Halloween dance."

It doesn't matter what the question is, Jack slowly receives it, repeats it, and answers it.

It's a part of how he processes and it takes a bit to get used to. At least it took me some time not to jump at what sounded like a question posed.

It's hard to describe how I like Jack.

Because it's more than just liking him. I feel safe when I have Jack in class.

And it's not just his predictability that makes me feel this way. He averages about 16 seconds between repeating the questions, and another 16 seconds before answering.

And in those 32 seconds I am catapulted into the abyss. Time slows. This is time that Jack is using to build a platform that will reach all the way through his mind and his senses to the people around him.

32 seconds is *nothing*. It's the blink of an eye to travel distances like that.

And I know that if I wait right where I am, Jack will reach me.

There's so much comfort in that. There's so much trust.

It's something I know. And he knows that I'll wait for him.

One day a week I get 32 seconds with Jack, and in these 32 seconds I can finally relax.

All I have to do is wait.

One Time Only

The power lines like tethers laid across space and time delivered as the universe sometimes does so clearly not to be missed listen for the hiss just a change of pressure through an opening too small for hurricane force winds to knock down the door I'd never tell you what to do but me I'm battening down the hatches and buttoning up the buttons.

I, Eye

The eye, for all intents and purposes, is closed for business.

I licked the thread a hundred times but it does not un-fray itself under the determined mission of my tongue.

I find it rude and unruly.

Mostly my bones will whisper in voices that I can't make out. The din from the penthouse usually wins, fueled by decidedly un-godlike fruit and a beautiful view.

This weeping bag that holds 25 feet of rope never learned about the miracle of train trestles, and no matter what they say there's only so long one can walk around with a piggy pink sack of screaming bones before someone calls the cops.

Or makes a cutting remark.

Same difference.

The eye is closed, I can tell by the thread. So we take up our forgotten knitting projects, soothed by the clicking of overlarge needles in a overquiet room.

And if we are very very lucky there may even be a view.

Falling Fruit Season

Such a long leash you have. The better to lead you with. The better to get tangled, but with fewer panic attacks. The power of a 'maybe' the power of an 'if only'.

The fruit falls from the tree with a resounding thwap.
　It hits the top of my car and I look around for someone to be mad at because it scares me.

I'm sorry I've been so hard to be with lately.

He has a brain tumor and he could die in a year, or he could live a perfectly long time. I asked him why he was still working at a job he hated and he laughed at me. "I have a family to feed". He cocks his head sideways, realizing that I thought he was a millionaire just because he worked six days a week nine to five for the last twenty five years to life.
　Oh. I guess I thought...doesn't matter I thought wrong.

He's got payments to make on his gold chains, just $5 a week, that's $20 a month and these gold chains could be all yours.
　But not the property, that belongs to the banks. The newest testament, like all the others, remains to be gathered from glossy

brochures in the lobby.

The Apocrypha were lost to us, just like the Book of Mary, (no not That one the Other one) giving out pedicures for free to get that foot spa off the ground.

Our Apocrypha, evolved as we are, the protests that made the news, a whole hundred days of toy soldiers then the police union said "okay sure" and then that man came into my house while I was sleeping and the cops never came.

Take that.

But the man who broke into our house, he wasn't a man, he was just a boy with too much cologne that dropped his phone in the yard.

That's why we don't call the cops, but you can trade it in for any new phone, doesn't matter what shape it's in. They're collecting precious metals.

So anyway back to these golden chains, they're still in your cart, you still have time, but the fine print says they don't leave the property, wrapped around everyone except your dog, who you keep on a long leash, but he's a good boy and minds. What would you do without him? As far from the wolf as could be, wouldn't know how to kill a rat, gentle as a dormouse.

What's the point of a door when it leads back to the lobby when it leads to the street filled with carts filled with gold that can't leave the parking lot?

I don't want to look at you. Don't look at me.

A Special SOB

Every universe starts with a dream
    With a cell with a quark with a spark.
    Nothing was made in the "you could do better"
Nothing was built in the "you should know more"
Everything is messy
Imperfect
And strange
this city was built
Exactly the same
With plenty of assholes
bearing their weight, asking
"now how is it you think You're so damn special"
And through a hardening mask a mumbled, "well I kind of thought we both were".

So let's do this thing already.

The State of the Garden

It's a prey-eat-prey world smothered in a heart-stopping helping of cloying love.

Why does everything I eat taste like dirt?

Pardon me, I meant rich soil.

The notion of dead heading made me cry.

"You were always so painfully sensitive". Yes. Your email found me and held me the way you never could.

Strangled by this chain link of language, beautifully expressed excuses first, sort the bodies later, we keep in step with best intentions, the ignorant beasts that they are.

Tripping over our robes. Too impatient for a proper fitting.

The oxygen masks only drop in first class, so kiss me you fool, you look good enough to draw breath from.

Your mouth tasting like that good New Jersey acid rain dirt.

I just learned that spiders sometimes use fireflies as bait, wrapping them up just enough for the light to draw bodies to the floor.

And that's the state of the garden.

Deviled Eggs

And this morning, such quiet, as I've never heard. Not in this house.

They sit in the living room, talking to each other, sharing news about people they know. My dad is telling stories about when my sister and I were babies. My mom is laughing and making breakfast.

My dad recounting a time when my sister and I were little.

We used to sit in the sandbox and dig and dig and dig, imagining that if we kept digging we'd get some place completely new.

I remember feeling excited and determined, that if we kept going we would discover something unknown.

My sister called it Digging For Devils.

That's what my dad is talking about now.

That and the tours I used to give whenever we went to a new

place, beckoning the family to follow me. The tour guide.

A reel my mom sent my dad.

Martin Luther King Day. My sister pronounced it Marthda Luthda King.

How he would be rolling in his grave if he were alive today. Like my dad's dad. Who hated nazis and loved America.

Digging For Devils.

I sit, without the benefit of the cursed television blaring, my mind thinking over my troubled dreams, trying to connect everything together.

Instead I have the one clear image of my sister and I sitting in a sandbox alone, coordinating our strategy, and my mind lets go of everything else.

Digging for Devils.

Reddy to Go

I am woman, hear me roar, Helen Reddy on the record player while we danced around the living room in my mom's high heels, laughing. So funny. Before the bloom before the long harsh summers. We were looking in the opposite direction, prepared for a frost not the choke of weeds that blocked out the sun dried out caught fire burned and burned.

We drowned once, on the Atlantic shore, pulled in rolled into a little ball of human sushi knees bloodied on the sand. When you're a child it's a million lives, running to tell an adult that you almost died and then realizing that someone took your bucket of Barbies.

A whole damn bucket of Barbies. Even the ones whose heads you shaved.

What the fuck. There's some little girl out there with MY Barbies living her best life.

Nothing stung as bad as that, not even the phone call from the doctor with there's no reason to panic but we found something abnormal not even the wages lost from all the teaching I had to do off the clock on how to pull your punches. (maybe as much as that)

The echoes of that song as it bounces down the long dark tunnel gaining only distance, our laughter all tangled up in it, gleeful and mocking.

Do you even know how much Barbies cost?

How Are You?

I'm afraid my radio silence is the sound of me swinging back and forth between paralyzed horror and corrosive overthinking. The way sounds cease to compute when there are too many of them. I'm afraid more and more.

Maaaaaaaan don't bother asking how I'm doing if you're not ready to hear the answer. There's a million other things you can say "good to see you hope you're well" but keep your inquiries to yourself cause I'm tired and I don't mean I didn't get enough sleep I mean no matter how much sleep I get I'm sick because we messed up and steeped ourselves in the poison so now I'm tired because my blood ain't right and ALSO I haven't been sleeping I'm tired of men masquerading as feminists who can't stomach a No fragile and wielding anger like a righteous tool sick and slick from the knives you don't even know you're holding I'm tired of my own internalization of weakness like a brain implant that doesn't come loose no matter how many times I slam my face against the wall and I'm tired of the dog and pony show in some kind of neon hellscape blinking lights and for profit fights everybody sick brained laying in a cage but I'm tired of working so hard all the time even when I'm not working and I'm tired of holding space for you and I'm tired of you not holding space for me and I'm tired about hearing about how you're tired EVERYONE'S TIRED and I'll wake up tomorrow and find a decent expression for my face to settle in and try again but don't ask me to lie to you about it because I have enough strength for everything thrown at me and more except for that one thing so let's skip it because I have a nap with my name written on it and a cat who never asks questions let alone questions they don't want the answer to.

I'm fine. How are you?

The suspiciously familiar song of the Marsh Wren

The Marsh Wren makes a sound from a dream I had so many years ago. In my grandmothers treasure-filled basement of her row home apartment in Philadelphia where she died, with her cats and her cactus garden. Amongst her paintings and yarn and knick knacks and boxes, I found an instrument made of long, grey rectangles, held together by material of some kind. Like the sound of stones sighing as they tumble through time.

If river water sang.

Maybe the dream was pieces from things I'd heard and seen, but nothing I can recall. The dream is vivid though. One of those dreams that feels more like a remembering, even though I was the only one there, wading through as I so often did in my waking life, playing with wooden toy soldiers and nesting eggs, the smell of old books and acrylic paint.

A day after parting with another bag of blood, my brain ignorant as to how my body is making so much of it, this dream memory is drawn up.

Some people think we choose everything that happens to us. That bad things only happen because we have more lessons to learn. I don't know about that. Or anything.

I love it here. I know that. I remember that. Even though sometimes I'm lonely in a way that has nothing to do with the company or lack thereof.

And I find it beautiful in a way that makes my heart quicken. That the marsh wren has a song that reminds me of an instrument from a dream that sounds something like a river rocks' song. On the day my grandmother would have been 90.

If river rocks could sing. If we could hear them.

Another Poem About My Hair Leave Me Alone And I'll Stop Writing Them

You can fuck right off about my hair.

Don't worry, I understand you have an opinion about the pleasingness of my appearance.

As far as you're concerned, I'm a Demon Bitch Brat Bat from Hell. Uuuugly and past my prime. No good.

And you can fuck right off about my skin. My Eyes. My Weight. My Shape. My Tits. My Clothes. And especially my hair.

My gall? You can have a field day with that.

But my hair?
   It's a nest for birds.
   A trash can for the gods chewing gum.
   It's the place I will snag on a branch on my way down to the sea and my body will hang there until I'm only bones, a Halloween decoration. A laughing skull as sailors crash their boats into the cliffside.

Only then do I suspect that you will properly fuck right off about MY FUCKING HAIR.

Our Damndest

Tube tube to be sure we share the why we share not just the good it's important too brother the show is good it's good it's great it's fine you know to know that most of the moments are not the best moments and that's okay hold up pal there's a face here you hear you forgot about it because you weren't looking it's okay you can't see everything all at one time but you can try and I always said in the flurriest moments I have two eyes and two ears and one mouth and the rest was implied it wasn't a lie just because I never said it all but just because you never asked no I wasn't asking but there's the truth of it and if you want to split hairs it's your splinter but the skin is mine so that leaves us where exactly where we left off, shake it off and do yer best boy-o nobody ordered the mess but we split the bill cause we're doing our damndest to be decent here.

We're doing our damndest to be decent here.

It's a Stranger World

Stephanie Strange has been making music in the Pacific Northwest for some years with her band Strange & the Familiars. She has been doing therapy every week since her first poetry book came out and you'll notice that her outlook hasn't gotten much better. But this book IS bigger than her first one, so there you go.

After leaving the food service industry she taught art and music to adults with I/DD and discovered that she was one of these adults and also that most of the people she knew were these adults. She writes poetry, performs shadow puppetry with her world building storytelling music project, complains loudly, and naps often.

She self-published her first book of poetry in 2024, and two comic books with illustrator Jay Reynolds because she gets sad when nobody wants to publish her work. She lives in Portland, Oregon and has a cat named Noxious Tyrannous Strange who does not like to be kissed or held like the baby he is.

She likes, loves, and is fully invested in the Oxford comma. She can't, won't, and will not turn back now.

For more writing you can become a patron at
www.patreon.com/stephaniestrange

Follow the music @strangeandthefamiliars

www.ingramcontent.com/pod-product-compliance
Lightning Source LLC
Chambersburg PA
CBHW071246070526
44583CB00017B/2355